A Christmas Homicide

A. TWISTED

Acknowledgements

I want to give a loving thank you to my Mom for always putting my brother and myself before her, and her needs. Without you, my dreams wouldn't be possible.

Trigger Warnings

Course Language, Spousal Abuse, Murder, Body Tampering.
Cheating, Anxiety and Depression. Read at own risk.

Contents

Hot Chocolate

Snowballs whizzed past my face at lightning speeds, while my three kids toppled over the walls of my hastily made fort.

"Aha!"

"You're mine!"

"Surrender now! And live to see tomorrow!" They yelled over one another as each one landed with an oof.

I pulled myself to my feet, peeling each child off me before bolting from the snowy enclosure.

"You'll never stop me!" I wailed, tossing the last of my frozen ammunition. When my arms were empty, each of my offspring stood, popping up from behind the snow wall like moles begging to be whacked.

It was eerie, yet impressive, the way they moved as one. Elli, my youngest at the age of four, made more snowballs and divided them amongst her siblings. Shawn, my eight-year-old, filled his arms and stood between me and his sisters. He tossed a snowball into the air and caught it, never breaking his daring stare.

A shiver crawled up my spine, and not due to the frigid air, as Georgia, my six-year-old, giggled maliciously. She stepped out from behind her brother, fully loaded, and ready to unleash.

"You can still surrender," Shawn grinned.
Obviously, that was my best option, but what kind of mother would I be if I didn't teach my children how to stand their ground?

"Never!" I raised my shoulders over my ears and readied myself. My fiery red hair bunched up around my face, tickling my nose, as I twinkled my wool-covered fingers.

Without warning, Elli pointed at me and yelled, "Fire!"

Arms swung; balls rushed through the air. I weaved, ducked, and dodged most of the shots thrown my way, but there was no avoiding them all. Before I knew it, I was being clobbered from every angle.

Shawn moved to my right; Georgia, to my left. Together, they pelted me with icy handfuls until I crumbled on the ground.

I thought about begging for mercy. To cry out for pity in hopes they would stop, but the only way to end the mayhem was to play dead. So, of course, I laid down and stuck out my tongue in an exaggerated corpse pose.

Everyone laughed and dogpiled on top of me. I wrapped my arms around my world and rolled from side to side as I squeezed them tight.

When I released my grip, Shawn got to his knees and jabbed his hands into my ribs in an attempt to tickle me. Not even the thick-down jacket I wore could save me from his bony knuckles.

I winced but did what I could to play it off, and quickly asked about hot chocolate. Each of their faces lit up, and they all went running for the house. I, however, laid there catching my breath.

"Phew, I'm getting too old for this." I sighed as I got to my feet.

· · · ● ● · ● · · · ·

The kettle whistled just as I pulled it off our gas stovetop and started pouring four steaming mugs. The marshmallows that the kids tossed in floated to the top and danced around in their chocolatey baths.

My three bouncing babes fiddled eagerly when I brought their drinks to the breakfast nook. Their winter gear hung from the fireplace which separated the kitchen from the den. It dripped steadily as the snow and ice melted away, and the fabric warmed.

"Be careful. It's hot." I warned each of them before taking my seat, and gently blowing on mine.

They followed suit; except for Elli. She fanned her vigorously while glaring like a fiend. She was always my eccentric one. Since about three days old, when she made a 'what you talk'in about' face to her father, I knew she was going to be a handful.

Georgia was the polar opposite; she was patient and shy. She blew on her hot chocolate and waited for it to cool, smiling at me as she did.

Then there was Shawn. My little man. The day he was born, he lifted his head all on his own. He has been strong-willed ever since.

These were my babies. They were my everything. I'd spent the last nine years focusing my life around them. Curating my time to suit their needs over mine. All so they could grow up to look more and more like their father.

Each one was blonde with hazel eyes and beaming smiles. Their voices were sweet and smooth, and easy to listen to. Then again, I could be biased...

Yes, I know how obnoxious I sound. I was you ten years ago, rolling my eyes at the mother who was overly active in their children's lives. But I have no other choice. My husband made it very clear once we were married that I would quit my job to be with the children and make his house a home.

So, that's what I did, and I did it well.

At first, it felt like a vacation. A break from the nine-to-five grind. The older the children got, however, the less I needed to do.

There was a hobby or two I took on over the years, but nothing really stuck. Nothing brought me the same kind of satisfaction as raising children; being their life force, and teacher.

I took a warm sip of my hot chocolate and glanced over my growing mini-him's. They sipped their drinks and played with their marshmallows, oblivious to my internal struggle. Everything was perfect in their eyes. Which it was, sort of.

A sigh escaped my lips, causing Georgia to look up and frown curiously. She was always the intuitive one, and though I did what I could to hide my strife, she somehow always knew when something was wrong.

I smiled at her and went to shrug it off when the door to the garage opened. If there was a chance to steer her away from the problem, it vanished the moment her father walked into the room and I tensed up. He nodded at me and kissed each of the kids on the tops of their heads before heading to his office.

"Dinner will be ready in an hour, dear," I called after him, though he clearly ignored me. *Bastard...* I flinched when I noticed Georgia watching me like a hawk. Startled, I forced a new smile and took another sip of my hot chocolate.

$\mathcal{H}eartache$

"Good night, Baby" I cooed as I closed the third and final door of the night. My duties were pretty well done for the day, other than my last tidy, but that could wait. I needed to talk to my husband.

Our marriage was crumbling. I could feel it. I needed to see if he felt it too, and if he wanted to do something about it.

There were couples all around us falling to pieces, and somehow, we always came off looking solid. I wondered how it would look if we did separate. What people would say and if anyone saw it coming—or lie and say they did.

My heart ached at the thought of a broken home, but at the rate we were going, we were already in one. So, if we needed to call it what it was, over, then at least I did my part.

My white cotton socks slid across the polished oak floors as I skated my way through the hall, down the main stairs, and past the front door. The parlor was just off the foyer, opposite the formal living space.

I hesitated at the dual pocket doors, unsure of how to start this daunting conversation when I overheard him on the phone.

"It's Christmas... I don't care about that. It's the kids. I owe them-" He scoffed, "That's not why... You know what, fine! I'm not arguing with you. Set it up!" He slammed the phone down and grumbled to himself.

This is not a good time, I decided, taking a step back.

The last thing I wanted to do was poke the bear when he was already on edge. I'd learned the hard way long ago that it was best to leave him to sulk. Nothing I said would make it better, and I didn't have the energy to be berated.

I turned away from his office doors and noted a boot out of place. My eyes rolled, and I got to work cleaning up. Leslie, our housekeeper would be there in the morning, but the least I could do was get the big stuff. We were a team. Between the two of us, we kept this lovely manner in tip-top shape.

As I dawdled around the kitchen, I couldn't help but glance down the hall toward the office. The light was still on, shining out from under the door, and I heard the faint sound of a keyboard tapping away. I sighed. There was never going to be a good time to talk about ending a decade-long relationship. It was best to rip the band-aid clean off.

I dried my hands on my towel and folded it over the oven's handle before slinking my way to the hallway. The floor beneath my feet creaked, causing me to jump, although I'm not sure why. This was my house, after all. There was no need to sneak.

I stood upright and raised my chin, doing what I could to seem more confident than I was. Still, my feet didn't move much faster than a snail, and my hand hesitated to knock. I stood there—outside his office—for what felt like forever. My mind reeled over what to say, and how to say it: *Daryl, Dear? I don't feel loved in this relationship, and I don't think you do either...* No, no. *Daryl, I love you and the life we have built, but I am not in love with you...*

"Ugh, that's worse." I shook my head. *I know he's wanted this longer than me, so why am I the one doing the dirty work?* My hand finally raised and went to tap on the door when it opened.

Standing there, scowling, was my husband. His broad shoulders puffed up, and he held his chin high. He looked furious with his thin lips pressed in a fine line. The shirt he wore was unbuttoned, and his tie was loose, yet he held his jacket in his hand as if he were about to leave.

"I thought you'd be asleep by now." He said, crossing his arms.

"I was just about to go that way. I was wondering if you wanted to join me?" I lied.

"I can't. I left some important papers at the office. I need to go get them..." It was clearly a lie, but I smiled and pretended to not know his work was digital and could be accessed from anywhere.

"Another night." I lifted my shoulder in a weak shrug and turned toward the stairs. "Good night."

"Night." He said as he rushed out the door. It shut tight, and he locked it, leaving me there alone with the kids. Again.

I rolled my eyes and went back to the kitchen. There was a bag of cheesy popcorn and a bottle of wine, calling my name. With my goodies in hand—no glass needed—I ventured to the master suite and turned on a random flick to scroll to.

As it played in the background, I got caught up on my friends' socials. My best friend Kati was on Vacation in Bali, and I was living vicariously through her.

Daryl and I had the money to travel, and the kids were old enough to enjoy it now, but we never went anywhere. He did. He traveled everywhere for work, and before the kids, he took me with. Now that we have the added baggage—not like he would be in charge of them—he refused.

That wasn't the only thing he's started refusing. It'd been over a year since he so much as kissed me. In fact, he started sleeping in the guest room around six months ago. *He has to know that this is over...* I bit down on the sudden tears that burned my nose. As strong as I pretended to be, the idea of our marriage ending broke my heart.

He Did What?

"The bell rang five minutes ago. What the hell is taking so long." Amber, a mother I knew from school drop-off, complained. "I don't get it. They do this every day but if I'm late once, I bet that would be the day they were on time."

I didn't have anything to contribute to the conversation; I rarely did considering all she ever did was whine. So, I sipped on my coffee and nodded along, sometimes adding a *hmm*.

Today, she seemed to notice my mood and promptly called me out.

"What's your problem?" She turned to face me head-on.

"Huh?" I flinched, unsure of how to answer. There wasn't a chance in hell I was about to tell her about my marital strife. I wouldn't be out of the parking lot before every parent knew about it. I needed something else...

Rather than answer with a lie, I decided a half-truth would suffice.

"I'm exhausted. I didn't get much sleep last night; I've been having strange dreams." I took another sip of my warm drink and prayed the doors would open so that our conversation could be cut short.

"Kelsey had weird dreams right before she found out Chris was cheating," Amber blurted. "What are your dreams about?"

Again, I found myself not wanting to answer. Sure, I liked Amber, kind of. Honestly, she was just the only mom to talk to me. I have what's called a *resting bitch face* and was rarely approached.

This didn't mean I was going to make her my best friend. She talked too much about everyone but herself, and it was rarely about their achievements.

I needed to say something, though. Otherwise, my excuse wouldn't work and she would go off on her own tangent, I'm sure.

"I don't really remember my dreams. Only the feelings." I admitted.

"Weird." Amber shrugged.
Before she could say any more or pry any deeper, the doors swung open and kids of all ages burst from them.

Parents froze in place as children flooded the parking lot, finding their adults no problem. As each one collected their mini-thems, the parking lot emptied, and soon, there was no one left but me.

My entire body felt numb, my knees wobbled, and I nearly fell. *Where the fuck are my kids?*

It was against the rules—they tell you to call and go through the front—but as a few stragglers left the building, I slipped in through the side door. I went straight for Elli's class first, then Georgia's. There was no sign of the girls or their teachers. It wasn't until I was halfway to Shawn's class that I bumped into Mr. Compton, the principal.

"Mrs. Greer. How can I help you?" He asked, clearly puzzled by my attendance.

"Where are my kids? They didn't come out the side doors. Where are they?"

"Let's find out," He said, skipping into a sprint toward the front office. I followed close on his heels, doing what I could not to go into a panic.

We burst into the reception to find the secretary had already left for home. Mr. Compton grumbled about how she should be here until five but didn't let that stop him. He plopped down in her seat and quickly fanned through her notes while waiting for her computer to reboot.

It was probably only a minute, maybe two, but waiting for answers when all I wanted to do was scream, felt like an eternity.

"It's all three? Yes? That's promising." Mr. Compton suggested.

"How is that promising?" I lashed.

"It means wherever they are, they're together. It also means it's less likely to be an abduction. Have you talked to Mr. Greer? Maybe he picked them up."

"He wouldn't do that. He is a very busy man." As I said the words, Mr. Compton grinned and turned the computer screen to face me.

It was Shawn's file, and it said, 'picked up by Father at lunch hour'. Mr. Compton then flipped to Georgia's, then Elli's. They all said the same.

"It says here that-"

"Right, of course," I said, cutting him off. "Thursday, yes. I-I got my days mixed up." I lied through my teeth. *What the hell is going on?* "Thank you. Sorry to have troubled you." I said, leaving the room.

"You have a good night," he called after me.

·· • • • • • ··

I stepped back out into the icy cold air and darted home. We only lived a few blocks away, so naturally I'd walked there. Now I was running. Snow and slush slipped out from under my feet, causing my thirty-years-old hips to strain.

When I got back to the house, my cold, frantic hands fumbled with my keys. Only my car was in the drive, with no tracks in the snow to say Daryl's jeep was in the garage.

"Shawn? Georgia! Elli!" I screamed the moment the door clicked open. "Guys! Are you home!?"

I raced to the kitchen and grabbed the cordless phone off its hook. As I dialed Daryl's number, I went from one room to the next, slipping in the puddles caused by my boots. Again and again, I called for my babies, and every time I was met with silence. By the time I started up the stairs, the phone dialed through.

"Hey," Daryl said on the other line.

"What are you doing? Where are you?" I started to beg.

"You've reached Daryl. Please leave a message after the tone." I growled and squeezed the phone in a rage fit. *Argh! Fucker!*

I didn't understand it. What was he doing? What was his plan? Did he expect to be home before I went to the school, or did he want to freak me out? Nothing about any of this made any sense. It was all highly out of character. In all our years of marriage, he didn't so much as lift a finger toward the domestic duties. So why now?

I went to the formal sitting room and flopped down on the couch. The coat I wore bunched up around my shoulders, covering my chin and making me breathe hot air into the already hot jacket. I quickly unzipped it and peeled it off my back.

"It's OK," I told myself. "Everything will be fine. It's not like he would ever hurt them..." As I reassured myself I couldn't help but wonder. I'd seen the late-night news segments about that father who killed his family—small children included.

There was no telling who a person was until they crossed that line. It didn't matter how long you were together, anything can happen.

Honey, We're Home

Tears poured down my face as the sunset. I'd already called the police, but with them being with their father and no reason to suspect foul play, they weren't going to do anything to help. So, I was left there to wallow until someone walked through the door.

I took off my boots and left them to soak the carpet and stain it with salt. My coat was tossed on the couch and my gloves and scarf were on the coffee table. If it'd been any other day I would have put them where they belonged, but right now I couldn't care less.

I laid curled up on the couch, watching the phone. *What if they got in an accident? I should call the hospital,* I decided, sitting up. As I reached for the phone, the front door opened and my home was filled with laughter.

All three of my angels trotted past with cotton candy, frozen syrup on a stick, and lolly-pops the size of their faces. They flashed wide smiles under bright red noses as they took off their winter gear, boosting about their day at the winter festival.

"That's wonderful." I faked a smile and helped them undress. "Oh wow. I'm so glad... Now off to bed with ya's. Shawn, help Elli, please. I need to talk to your dad."

The moment the kids were up the stairs and around the corner, I turned on my husband and sneered.

"Who the fuck do you think you are?!" I scream-whispered. "You can't just sign them out halfway through the day and take off without telling anyone!"

"Sure I can," He scoffed. "And I believe I just did." Daryl clenched his jaw and crossed his arms, daring me to test him.

I swallowed deep and puffed out my chest, matching his bold stance. A moment of tense silence passed between us. There was no denying this would be our biggest fight yet, and I couldn't help but shake that he did it on purpose.

I narrow my eyes and choose to hold my tongue. It wasn't worth the hassle. I was just happy to see my kids home and in one piece.

"Mom," Shawn's voice echoed from the top of the steps. "Elli won't brush her teeth."

"Duty calls." I hissed.

"Best get to it. Though I doubt they will sleep any time soon." He grinned and went to his office, closing the doors behind him.
***

Getting the kids to bed was easier than expected. Each one crashed quickly due to the overabundance of processed sugars. Elli complained of a tummy ache, but it was nothing a little bread and water couldn't settle.

Once they were all cozy in their beds, I headed downstairs to my husband's office. I was done watching my temper and needed to get everything off my chest. Not only the kidnapping but the distance he's caused, the stress-filled nights of yelling and berating me for no reason other than him being in a bad mood. The obvious affairs and blatant disrespect for me.

I was done! And it was about time he heard about it.

My fist rose up to slam into the wooden door, but my gut dropped and I froze. I wasn't sure why; it was almost like the universe wanted me to listen.

"...I thought she would have by now" Daryl whispered. "That's not how this works. She has to end it... No. If I end it, I owe her half of everything plus, plus, plus... According to the prenup, I need her to end it... without finding out about you."

Too late, I thought. *Cat's out of the bag.*

My arm dropped to my side, and I slouched. I always assumed he had a mistress. Something told me it was true, but I didn't care. My sex drive was next to none since before Elli. Not feeling obligated to satisfy my husband was a gift in my eyes.

It was the idea that he wanted to end it all while leaving me high and dry after so many years of sacrifices; that's what did me in. *You son of a bitch!* All these years I'd seen other housewives be ruined, left to fend for themselves after decades out of the workforce. I always believed Daryl would never be that way with me.

My heart raced, and my head spun. Drool filled my mouth, and I thought I might faint. As I fought to calm my nerves, Daryl laughed and caused them to spike all over again. It didn't seem to matter what I did; even stepping away didn't help. If anything it made things worse not being able to hear what was being said.

I began to pace outside the door while taking deep breaths. *What do I do?* Clearly, he wants me to go in there ragging. He wants me to end things so he can toss me out with the trash.

I wasn't about to let that happen, though. If he wanted this marriage over, he needed to end it.

So, instead of knocking or barging in like a crazed lunatic; I went back upstairs to *my* master suite and went to sleep in *my* bed.

Here To Stay

I treated this Friday like any other. It started with getting myself, and kids ready for the day. Then it moved on to school drop off, before the weekly grocery shop, lunch with my mother, and back to the school for pick up.

Now I was trapped at Shawn's Taekwondo class for at least an hour.

I wasn't too sure how Daryl spent his Friday, but I can tell you his Thursday didn't go to plan. Not with the way I walked away. He didn't seem too affected by it this morning when he ate his breakfast and left for work. If anything, he seemed his normal bland self. Not a guilty bone in his body.

Most would tell me to be more bothered, to get a lawyer, but Daryl's family had money. If they wanted, they would bury me in legal debt, and I'd not only be divorced, I'd be bankrupt. The most I would do with a lawyer is look into my rights, and even then, it's not like I can leave.

My best course of action was to settle in. I mean, even if we did split up it's not like I would change much about my lifestyle.

If anything, I might get a job to keep myself busy. I sure as heck wouldn't be out dating or partying like so many other mothers do—which, no judgment. All the power to them. I was just never one to do such things, even when I was young.

Staying married to Daryl while he satisfied himself elsewhere seemed like a fair trade for the lavish life he'd given me. Not to mention the life he will continue giving our children. It would be whomever was on the phone the other night, that may cause an issue. In which case, he can end things and deal with the consequences.

A smile trickled across my face as I sat there, watching my son's high-kick. Georgia sat at my feet doing her homework, while Elli laid with her legs up the wall, watching something on YouTube—though I'm not sure how she heard anything over the echo of the school's gymnasium.

Other parents chattered to pass the time. Myself included. In fact, I was slightly proud of myself for branching out and joking with a fellow mom. It was a new side of me, and I wanted to see more of it.

When practice finally came to a close, I was met by the instructor. He followed Shawn like a puppy to where I stood. A tall, dark, and handsome puppy. I crossed my arms and waited to hear about Shawn's latest smart-mouth remark. There was no denying he was hilarious, but the boy needed to learn about when and where it was appropriate.

"Ms. Greer?"

"Mrs." I corrected, though I'm not sure why.

"Oh, Mrs. Greer." He said shyly. "My name is Hank. I'm Shawn's instructor. I got to tell you, Shawn is a true talent. I would love to sign him up for a competition."

"Really?" I beamed. "OK, Shawn? What do you think?"
He shrugged, clearly unsure of what to do.

So I stepped in and deflected for him. "Well, we will have to talk to your Father, and see what he says."
Shawn smiled and nodded, knowing that was my excuse to get out of things.

"Sounds like a plan." Hank smiled. "See you next week, sport."
He ruffled Shawn's hair and went to tidy the mats.

··········

On the drive home, I couldn't help but swoon over the way that man talked to Shawn. It was the way I wanted Daryl to speak to him. Sadly, it was always a competition with him, and unless Shawn came out on top, his father wasn't happy.

It was likely why the idea of a competition upset him. I mean, why would you want to compete with a father like his? It didn't matter how high I boosted his spirits, Daryl always found a way to crush them.

I should have left his ass years ago. I could have made due. Gone back to work; something. It would have been one thing being a couple of years out of the workforce, with one mouth to feed, but over a decade with three—absolutely not. I would never survive, and I wasn't about to raise my children in poverty. Not if I could help it.

I looked through the rearview mirror at my girls and instantly felt guilty. *No, I wouldn't change a thing.*

"Hey, mom?" Shawn peeped from beside me.

"Yea, baby?" I asked, turning into our driveway.

"We're not really going to ask Dad about the tournament. Are we?"

"No, baby. Even if you decide to try out, we don't have to tell him," I promised.

"Really?" He nearly jumped from his seat. He was so happy.

"Pinky swear." I held out my hand, and we locked pinkies. "Now, it's time for bed. Let's go." I told the lot of them.

After some complaints, a bedtime snack, and some begging to sleep with me, I got them all to sleep. In their own beds. It was then time to do my nightly duties and go to bed myself.

As I finished up, I noticed Daryl's office light was still on. He was gone for the next few days *'for work'*, or so he said. I debated on leaving it on; he hated me entering his space. Especially when he isn't around to keep me from snooping. *It could be a trick. A reason to fight when he gets home...* Or it could be my opportunity to get and look around.

I crept down the hallway, tip-tocing as if anyone were around to hear me. It didn't matter that I knew the room was empty; I froze when I finally made it to the doors.

If I went in there, I needed to leave everything as it was. The man was overly particular and noticed when things were centimeters out of place. That also meant that if I found anything, I needed to leave it there. Then again, what did I plan to find? The prenup? I had my own copy of it somewhere.

Still, my hand lifted and touched the door. *Here we go,* I hmm'd to myself.

The door clicked and slid open slowly. It creaked as it did, adding an eerie tone to the already risky invasion. I took a step into the pristine room, untouched by mine or the kid's hands—Only Leslie was permitted to clean in here. The polished floors glistened under the overhead light, so clean you could eat off it. Much like the other surfaces in the room.

Yes, I kept a clean home, but this room looked straight out of a magazine. The desk sat in the center of the room with two decorative chairs in front, positioned for meetings he never held. Floor-to-ceiling shelves lined the back wall, filled with books he'd never opened. There was a bar cart, a standing globe, and even a chaise for lounging by an electric fire place.

I rolled my eyes. I had a nook upstairs, called my craft corner. The mayhem in that small six-by-six square kept me from enjoying the arts. *If I had a room like this, I would never stop making things.*

I stepped deeper into the room, gliding my hand along the back of a chair. Like the rest of the room, everything on his desk had a place. His laptop was shut with a folder on top. Above it, near the edge was a cup of pens, a photo of the kids, and a miniature statue of a bull plated in gold. Tacky thing if you ask me, but he loved it.

None of those things caught my attention, though; it was his day planner sitting next to the laptop that caused me to pause. It was left open, with a gold pen on top. *I wonder if he tracks his dates...*

I dragged my feet over to the desk and peered down at the past week. Each day was cram-packed with meetings at the office, at lunch, and even dinner meetings. There was nothing about the women I knew he saw on the side, but there was nothing scheduled for Christmas either, and I knew for a fact he was making plans. *I wonder... If I can prove he's cheating, that should void our prenup... That must be why he doesn't want me to find out about her.*

I chewed my bottom lip and fanned through the pages. Still, there was nothing mentioning dates with other women. *He must be another planner.* Then again, if Daryl was smart, he would keep that information in his head. Too bad for him, I knew he couldn't remember anything to save his life.

I thought to check his laptop, but I knew there would be a password, and I didn't know it. Nor did I know what would happen if I tried too many times. I wasn't exactly tech-savvy. Nearly anything electronic broke after I used it. So, I flipped the planner back to how I found it and went to leave, keeping the light on when I did.

With no new information or evidence to use against Daryl, I headed up to my room. *Maybe that's what I should do*, I thought to myself as I passed my kids' rooms and slinked into my own. *I'll get myself a P.I and build a case against him. While they do that, I can play the perfect little housewife. Once we have proof of his infidelity, I should get my divorce.* A smile crossed my face as I settled into my bed. Of course, my plan wasn't ideal. I should be free to leave when I want without the stipulations; but having a goal was better than being in limbo.

Happier Days

The coming weeks passed like any other. I slept alone in my bed, kept a clean house, and ignored my husband and his late-night ventures. It wasn't hard living life like normal, only now I had a bit more of a *'who cares'* attitude.

I no longer shied away from buying myself pretty things, or new toys for the kids. I even got myself a babysitter so I could go to the movies all by myself, and ate a hot meal *all by myself.* I was loving it, and Daryl had yet to mention or even notice a difference.

Then again how would he? In my newly discovered freedom, he had his own. I was no longer asking questions, or pestering to rekindle things. I wasn't even arguing when he was late, or flat-out skipped family dinners. He was practically a free man, and we were both happier for it.

Though I knew it would be short-lived. Soon, my bill for my lawyer would come in, and when—if—he saw it, he was going to flip.

See, over the last few weeks, I contacted our family lawyer and learned my rights—which were in abundance.

Turns out Mr. Greer and his mistress overlooked some things in their greedy search to ruin me. Like our child clause; for each child, I am entitled to one million a year in support. That didn't even include the alimony payments. Oh, and don't get me started on the infidelity clause. *Ha!* If I can prove he's unfaithful, this buffoon owes me half of everything plus, plus, plus. *Fool.*

With such stakes, you'd think he would have tried harder to work things out, but not my Daryl, no. He was used to getting everything he wanted, with no repercussions. It was a trait I heavily hated in him. His lack of accountability was astonishing. Even in the early days of our relationship, he was never in the wrong. *God, why did I even marry you?*

He was charming, I'll give him that, and he spoiled me something fierce. Which was something I'd never experienced before. Still, I can remember thinking he was a pompous rich kid. My best friend at the time hated him too. So, how did I end up with a ring on my finger and his seed in my belly?

Speaking of seed, I was stuck at yet another taekwondo meet with both girls at my feet. In the new year, Georgia starts her dance class and Elli has her beginner's art course. Once again, there would be no time for me. Like every year before, I was about to be overrun by extracurriculars.

I could always get a nanny with my millions, I grinned, but that wouldn't be for some time yet. For now, I needed to sit tight and daydream about my future.

"Mommy, I'm bored," Georgia whined, prompting Elli to join in.

"Yes, yes," I said, hushing them while looking at my phone for the time. "Ten more minutes, then we can get some ice cream" They beamed at the offer and went back to entertaining themselves.

When practice came to a close, Shawn came running over-excited about something. I leaned over, arms wide and ready to accept him.

"What's going on?" I asked, squeezing him tight.

"I'm going to compete in that tournament." He said, pulling away and jumping up and down.

"You are?! That's wonderful!" I gushed.

The girls giggled and joined in his excitement before telling him about our ice cream stop. All three shouted louder, drawing attention from the other families.

"Coach Hank says if I practice, I could get a trophy," Shawn beamed.

"Then you better get to it. When is it?" I pointed to his shoes, silently telling him to get ready to go.

He sat on the floor to put them on, "Two weeks." He said nonchalantly.

"Two week?!"

"Yes, it's the Christmas tournament, and he will be competing with the other first years—it's more of a display than anything else," Hank added from over my shoulder.

I nearly jumped out of my skin. I didn't notice him standing there; I was too fixated on my bouncing babes.

"Jesus!" I snipped, gripping the collar of my jacket. "Sorry, I, uh. I didn't see you." As I sorted myself out, Hank told me more details while handing me a consent form. "Thank you," I said, taking the paper. "We will be there."

"Wonderful. There is a secondary practice and a rehearsal next week. See you then." he flashed a sly side smile, causing my knees to weaken.

Oh, hello there. Long time no tingle, I grinned at my loins.

Elli yanked on my arm, drawing my attention away from the handsome man to remind me of my promises. I assured her that we were going and took one more glance at the tight buttocks of Shawn's mentor.

The fact I would be single soon seemed to awaken something lost within me, and apparently, I wanted Hank to find it.

Hank-y Panky

Ice cream so late wasn't the greatest idea. Elli wound up with an upset stomach, and Shawn's excitement over his up-and-coming show was amplified. It made it rather difficult to get them to sleep, but when they were down, they were out.

Once free of my mini-me's, I took care of my evening tasks, sipping off a dry gin as I piddled around. Things went by quickly enough, but before I knew it, it was 9:30 PM, and I was exhausted.

I topped off my glass and headed upstairs. A piping hot shower was calling my name, so I went to my bathroom and started the water. Steam coated the mirror as I stripped down and stepped into the glass box.

The hot water drenched me, warming me to the core. I leaned back and soaked my hair, then face before grabbing my loofah and dabbing a glob of body wash on top. It lathered and coated my body in suds as I scrubbed the day off my skin.

Once I was clean, I leaned on the wall and switched the shower head to the rain setting. As the water trickled over my body, I couldn't help but think of Hank's smile. It flashed before my eyes again and again as other images of his muscular hands and broad shoulders joined in. Without warning, the tingle between my legs was back.

It'd been quite a while since I felt the need. I'd blamed it on post-partum depression, like most moms suffered. Now I wondered if it was just the dick available to me. I bit down on my lip and tickled my lower abdomen with my left hand, circling my belly button seductively.

I wonder what Hank has hanging, I smiled, thinking of the visible bulge when he wore his uniform. Or the glimpse I got this past summer at the beach. I was with the kids, and he came out of the water to say, hello. His sopping wet shorts clinging to him in all the right places, giving the whole crowd ample time to gawk.

I closed my eyes and slipped my hand lower until my fingers met my lips. They stopped just above, hesitant to go further. Not only had it been years since a man touched me, it'd been longer since I touched myself. With the way childbirth warped my body, I felt disgusting. The way my libido wanted to take over now, shocked me.

I took a deep breath and brought my right hand to my mouth, chewing on my index fingernail. *I shouldn't, I'm still a married woman,* I told myself.

It was clearly an excuse. My marriage was over, and even if it wasn't, it's not like I was going out and physically touching another man. It was all in my head. No harm, no foul, right?

Regardless of the logistics, I turned around and switched off the water. The mood was ruined, and I was beyond ready for bed.

As I crawled into my sheets, I clicked on my phone and turned off tomorrow's alarm. It was Saturday after all, and I was fine with sleeping in. *Let Elli wake me up when she's ready,* I grinned.

There was a brief urge to scroll, but there wasn't much point tonight. I could barely keep my eyes open. So, I shut off my phone and plugged it in to charge.

My exhaustion meant nothing. Not with the way my mind reeled over Hank and his low voice, thick fingers, and buff arms. I wondered what it would be like to have them wrap around me as he whispers sweet nothings.

I swallowed deeply and sifted under my covers to lay flat on my back. Before I knew it, my legs were spread and my hand was back to where it ventured in the shower. His imaginary sweet talk turned dirty as my fingers twirled around the nub below the hood. Shivers ran up my spine as the slit between my legs turned wet.

Fake kisses tickled my neck as he moved down my body. I followed the sensation with my other hand, causing goosebumps and bringing my fantasies to life. With both hands hard at work, I focused my mind on Hank and the things I wanted him to do to me.

I wanted his head between my legs. To have his tongue do what my fingers were trying to do. I slipped them lower, dipping my middle finger inside. A thrill rocked me, and I pushed deeper, adding another after a moment of pumping. I bent my knees and curled my toes. My right hand joined my left, rattling my bean and causing my back to arch.

Yes, Oh yes, Hank. I bit my lip to stop from squealing. It didn't take long before my legs kicked out, and I vibrated with exhilaration. Water gushed around my fingers as the quick, overwhelming orgasm took over my body.

Fuck me, I huffed, pulling my dripping hand out from under the blanket, wiping it dry. "I wonder if Hank can do that."

Hard Work Pays Off

The night of Shawn's tournament came faster than anyone could anticipate. It gave him very little time to get up to the same level as the others he would be alongside, but he did it. And he did it with ease. I couldn't help but be proud of him for his self-discipline. He practiced every night in his room, secretly showing me his progress as he went.

It broke my heart that he needed to hide this from his father to enjoy it. Their relationship shouldn't be strained—not this young, when he's still so innocent—father's and son's should be best friends. A united front. Not in competition. It made me hate the man more and more.

I wondered about the day they played hooky, and how happy Shawn looked when they got back. It was clear his dad could play nice when he wanted, making his competitiveness with our son more unnerving. Like he got a kick out of bringing Shawn down. *I need to leave this man, get Shawn far, far away.* Too bad, it was easier said than done. *Don't worry baby, I'll figure it out. I always do.*

While sitting there with my girls, cheering on their brother, I found myself glancing at Hank. He was fully dawned in a traditional dobok. The white uniform was synched at the waist by his black belt, and his feet were bare. His silky brown curls fell over the headband across his forehead, sporting the schools logo front and center.

Damn, you are a good-looking man, I thought while checking out his ass. My teeth tapped together lightly, eager to bite. As my perversions for the man slowly changed to images of single life, I wondered how I would navigate it all. I'd already established I wouldn't be the party type, but should I date?

A large part of me wanted to say no, to continue to focus on my kids and when they leave the nest, go from there. Another part–the part that watched Hank guide his team–wanted a man as family oriented as me.

My issue was, how do I initiate something like that? Do I go online like everyone else? *Ugh,* the idea of that made my skin crawl. I'd heard the stories. I knew all about the dating pool. Or, should I call it a swamp?

This made Hank even more enticing.

I put my foot on the bleacher bench in front of me. It bent my knee, giving my elbow a place to rest as I supported my chin. We'd been there an hour already, and there was still another to go.

The girls kept busy; Elli with her drawing, and Georgia with her dolls. I'd thought about getting them a sitter and letting them stay home, but I wasn't sure how late we would be. I didn't want Daryl to feel obligated to relieve them, then be *'stuck taking care of the kids'* until I got home.

I never understood his animosity toward our kids. They were pretty amazing. They rarely fussed, almost always listened, and were wickedly smart. We got very lucky with each and every one of them. Yet he couldn't be bothered. Hank could though.

After the tournament was said and done—and each of the beginners got their trophies—Shawn came skipping over, all smiles and bright eyes.

"Mom did you see?!" He waved his participation trophy.

"I did, I did." I smiled.

"One day, I'm going to get one of those," He added, pointing to the actual trophies given to winners. First place was as tall as him—possibly taller.

I raised my brows and smiled bigger, "I bet you will!"

"Sensei!" Shawn called over his shoulder, saying one of the many words he'd learned in the course. Hank turned around to look, smiling when he saw it was Shawn calling him over.

He said goodbye to the parents he was chatting with and made his way to us. I instinctively straightened my shirt and tucked my hair behind my ear. My lips folded between my teeth in an awkwardly tight grin.

"Shawn! That's what I'm talking about buddy!." They high-fived and Shawn did a few happy jumps. "Mrs. Greer," Hank added with a nod.

"Sen-see" I returned the respectful gesture as my face flushed. *That is not how you say that...* I wanted to palm my forehead from embarrassment. I shouldn't have said a word.

Luckily for me, he chuckled, unoffended by my lack of culture.

"Shawn did very well today. Better than some of my students who have been practicing all year. He has a true knack for the arts."

"He has a knack for everything." I smiled and nudged Shawn playfully.

"That he does. He gets it honestly, I'm sure." Hank smiled at me with a glint in his eye that weakened my knees.

Georgia, catching the looks between us, spoke up "We are going for ice cream, you should come."

All the blood left my face, and my fingers tingled. *What the hell?!* I thought. What was she doing? I took a deep breath. She was six; it's not like she understood the implications of inviting a man that's not her father on a family date. Or did she? I'd said no to ice cream after the last time. Was this her way of getting a treat?

As I went to excuse her and tell him not to feel obligated, I noticed his face light up.

"Yes, I would like that very much," He said before I could stop him. "Let me get changed and I will meet you in ten minutes?"

"Uh, yes, perfect." I stammered. Hank left us, and I gave Georgia a look, which she shrugged and grinned at.

It was a stunning night for December, so we decided to walk to the small café down the road. We smiled at one another as the children ordered, barely saying a word. On the walk from the community center to the shop was barely a block, and between the kids, we didn't get a word in edgewise. Now that they were busy, we were too shy.

At the register, he insisted on paying, making things feel even more like a date. I didn't argue, however. The last thing I needed was to draw attention to an already risky choice. We took a seat near a window overlooking the frozen park. Tongues licked, mouths slurped, and spoons scooped as Hank and I smiled some more, still not talking. It wasn't until the kids were full and off playing on a vintage pinball machine that Hank brought up Shawn.

It was nice to have someone to talk to who was as amazed by my children as I was. To hear him boast about my son's accomplishments with such gusto. It caused me to swoon. The more he spoke, the deeper my crush grew.

Soon the conversation got more personal; talking about desires, plans, and ideas. I believe we even flirted at one point.

"I've never met someone who gets ice cream in the dead of winter," Hank teased

"Clearly someone does, or else these guys wouldn't be open... Plus, if you take it with you, it doesn't melt right away," I explained

"Touche," He chuckled.

We talked for so long, it was closing time and well past my children's bedtime. So we tidied up our mess and got ready to go. As we did, our hands grazed, and I flinched back saying sorry.

Hank's carefree voice told me it was ok, but for some reason, I decided to think out loud:

"No, it's not. I'm a married woman. I shouldn't be out with you, not yet. Not until the papers go through."

"Mrs. Greer–"

"It's Jen, you can call me Jen." I huffed. My hands shook and my ears rang. *Why did I give him my first name? I should have kept it professional.*

"Jen," He corrected slowly. "It's not like this is a date. You've done nothing wrong..." He must have caught my face sink because when I didn't say anything, he asked: "Is it?"

"No, I'm married..."

"but you want it to be?" His eyebrows raised with excitement, which didn't help the matter–though it was comforting.

"What? I–Well. Wait." I didn't know what to say. I should have caboshed this the moment Georgia invited him. Especially after the other night's spicy fantasy.

"You want to date me?" He gave a sly side smirk and wiggled his brows.

"I–Ha!" I laughed out of humiliation and called my children over, "Time to go, get your jackets on."

"You don't have to worry Jen, I am a very patient man." You could tell he was holding back a laugh, but it wasn't in a taunting sort of way. He was playful–happy.

Oh god, I still have to walk back to my car with you.

He Knows

The next couple of days went rather smoothly, nothing of note really. The kids grew more and more anxious for Santa, and Daryl left early for yet another *work trip*, leaving us alone for the holidays.

Any other year, this would upset me and knowing what I know, it should upset me more, but I was content. Possibly even happy. The kids and I went on about our days as if nothing was missing. Which only encouraged my decision to leave.

The morning was long; boring. I got started on my weekend to-do's list while the kids occupied themselves. The girls were upstairs out of the way and Shawn was pigging out in the Den. *I swear that child never stops eating.* I thought about lounging, reading a book, and taking time for myself since Daryl wasn't here to complain, but Christmas dinner was just around the corner, and I was hosting.

My house was damn near immaculate to begin with, and I'd given Leslie time off until the New Year. Still, my Mother-in-law—though she's never touched a mop—loved to scrutinize my home if there was so much as a speck of dust floating. This prompted me to vacuum, dust, and have a quick phone call with my own mother while I cleaned the kitchen.

If I'd known it was going to be nothing but complaints, I would have picked music. Instead, I was trapped listening to her go on about *my* circumstances, always coming back to the day he took the kids without telling me.

"I hope he gets a thousand itches in places he can't scratch," is what she'd said. I'd tried not to laugh, but hearing such things come from her wrinkled mouth was too funny.

Even now—hours later—I chuckled at her snarky remarks. It made the idea of Daryl coming home next week less taxing. With the way our relationship was as of late, his time away couldn't last long enough. Heck, when he mentioned leaving town from the twenty-third until the New Year; I didn't bat an eye. I told him to do something for the kids and left it at that.

If I did bother to ask, he would have lied and said work anyway, so what's the point? For now, my ignorance was indeed bliss. Plus, he's missed Christmas Day every year since Elli was born. What would make a week this year any different?

The rest of the day went smoothly. The kids left at one point to play outside with the neighbor kids, only to come in frozen to the bone. I made them all soup for dinner and sent them off to bed before carting my own tuckus up the stairs.

I was glad the day was done, and that tomorrow seemed easy; less stressful. Ideas of what to do with the kids on our family Sunday came to mind as I got cozy in bed.

Dreamland was beckoning and my eyelids fluttered, but just as I started to drift off, the front door slammed open.

My entire body went cold as I paused to listen. *I locked it,* I told myself, and I had. During my final walk-through, I checked again. The house was locked up tight. *So, who the hell?* There was a slam and a bang, and I started wondering how the fuck I would get my kids out of the house and away from this new unknown danger. That is, until I heard the voice.

It was Daryl, and he was pissed.

He'd tossed his bag, knocking it off the small table that held our mail, and shouted—uncaring that the kids were fast asleep.

"Jen! Get down here! Now!"

Uh oh, I bolted from my room to meet him, grabbing my house coat on the way. It was barely tied at my waist when I reached the top step and cursed in a hushed voice.

"What is your problem! It's nearly midnight!"

"You. You are my problem!" He lashed, waving a set of papers. "You think I wouldn't find out? Who do you think gets the bill, bitch?"

"Excuse me?" I said, taking a step back. *Here we go. He's gotten the lawyer's bill.*

"You want to leave me, do you?"

"No," I answered, surprised by his fury. *I thought he wanted me to leave him...* "I just want to know my rights in case you leave me."

It wasn't a total lie. My intention wasn't to leave him, or at least, not at first. If he wasn't making his own plans behind my back, I never would've taken these steps.

"Bullshit!" He snarled, coming up the stairs. "I read this over and over! No way you're just planning ahead." He closed in on me, bringing his face so close to mine, our noses nearly touched. "If you think you're going to clean me out, you have another thing coming!"

"Clean you out? If you and your little mistress decide to take off, I'm taking what's mine."

"Get fucked, Jen! Yours!? None of this is yours!"

"According to the prenup; half of it is, and then some, if I can prove your girlfriend exists. Which reminds me, the bill for my P.I will be coming any day now." I went to turn and leave, but Daryl reached out and grabbed my arm, yanking me back to face him.

His eyes burned red, and he bared his teeth. I'd never seen him so angry—then again I'd never seen him not get his way. He dug his fingers into my skin and pulled me downward, contorting my body until I was forced to look up at him. I bit back the whimper that tried to escape my lips and glared at the man mistreating me.

"Let, go," I growled.

He leaned over, getting back in my face. "OK." With that, he flung me around and tossed me down the stairs.

My body flailed as I bounced off each step; bending and breaking on every corner. I hit off the railing where the stairs bent, knocking the wind out of me. Still, my body didn't stop moving. I went to cry out in pain, but when my face smacked off the marble tile, my world went black.

Head Wounds

I wasn't sure if it was the rustling of bags or the muttering that woke me, but there I was, forcing my sight back through a pounding headache.

I raised my hand to touch my forehead but winced before I even made contact. It's like my nerve endings knew better, leaving me to assume it was cracked wide open. The blood in my eye only solidified that fact. I moved my fingers to my eyes to rub them clean, but a thick flap of skin caused me to flinch and avoid my face altogether. I did what I could not to panic as I got my bearings.

Fuck me, I thought as the room came into focus. I was in the garage, next to the beer fridge, not far from our chest freezer. Daryl was bent over, digging through our frozen food, emptying it as he went.

"This will do, I'll put her in here and figure the rest out later, yea." He muttered to himself.

Put who in what? I wondered, my stomach flipping as the room started to spin. I leaned back and closed my eyes, doing what I could not to wretch everywhere. *What is he doing? What the hell happened? Where are my kids?* I didn't have the answers for any of it. The last thing I remembered was turning off my T.V, and rolling over to go to sleep. *Oh wait! He came in yelling.* I remembered.

I forced myself to look, to watch and see what he was up to when he took the last of the food out. He bagged it—not even bothering to save any of it—and turned back to me.

I instinctively closed my eyes and went limp, playing the part of a dead woman. Darly was too crazed to catch on and went to lift me into the freezer. I half expected him to say sorry, to treat me gently, but the jerk picked me up like a rag doll, complaining about how heavy I was and how this was fucking his whole plan up.

There was no remorse or sadness. Only a clear fear of getting caught and going to jail. I doubted he was even thinking of our kids at this point, and how he took their mother away from them. Nah. His focus was on getting my body into a cold place so that he could form a plan. Too bad for him, I wasn't one to go without a fight.

My relaxed body flopped in his arms, making it hard for him to maneuver me. He dropped me and grumbled to himself about being weak and needing to, *'get this done'*. While he was busy having a pity party, I noticed Shawn's baseball gear in a heap not far from me.

Before Daryl came back to pick me up, I reached out and grabbed the bat. As I did, he foolishly went to the beer fridge to get a cold one. With him distracted, I got to my feet and readied my swing. *You got one chance, make it count.* I told myself.

Daryl closed the fridge door and cracked the top of the bottle. As he took his swig, he glanced my way out the corner of his eye. The beer bottle slipped from his hand, shattering on the concrete floor. Daryl lifted his arms in surrender, but his eyes were filled with hatred. If I let him go, even now, he would only attack me again.

Knowing I was no longer safe with this man, I whacked him with the bat upside the head, causing his to split like mine. He stood there for a moment, his mouth open, his eyes dumb before falling half into the freezer, bent over with his ass in the air.

Blood dripped from his busted skull, with brains and hair mixed in. I moved to the side of the ice box to get a better angle and gave a courtesy whack just for good measure. The metal bat left a slight indent in the bone, making me smile with surety that he was dead—if not brain dead. Either way, he wasn't going to hurt me or the kids ever again. Not to mention my children were set for life with his life insurance payout.

For a split second, I was proud but was quickly dawned by the repercussions of what I'd done. I wasn't some rich white man, I wasn't about to get away with this with a slap on the wrist. They were about to throw the book at me.

"Oh shit. Oh shit!!" I dropped the bat, causing it to clank off the floor louder than I expected—or was that me hyper-focusing? Who knew. All I can say is everything around me was vibrant, and time seemed to slow.

I already knew what I was going to do without really processing it. The freezer was empty after all, and once the time was right, I would take it to the dump. I worked there as a teen and knew that if you drove your junk out far enough, no one would ever find it.

I stumbled over and lifted his legs, toppling the rest of his body into the freezer. There was more room than expected, and I didn't want so much food to go to waste, so I untied the garbage bags of frozen goods and put them back, burying him.

Once he was fully hidden, I closed the lid and went to grab boxes to place on top. As I did, my head throbbed, and I wondered how I was going to hide it from the masses. *Questions are going to be asked, and I better have my story straight.*

How He Did It

I'd barely slept last night and not because of the gash on my scalp. After cleaning myself up, it was clear the damage wasn't as bad as either of us expected. Head wounds bleed heavy no matter the extent of the injury.

The adrenaline of what happened wore off quickly, leaving me with nothing but dread over the consequences of my actions. I wonder what he would have done if I'd woken up and not attacked him. Would he have finished me off, or nursed me? Maybe take me to the hospital after convincing me to lie. Who knows?

Regardless, he was dead, and I was set to go to jail the moment someone found out. *That's fine,* I told myself. *As long as I get through Christmas. Then, I will get rid of him, and say he ran off with his whore...*

I spent the majority of the day in the kitchen—close to the door to the garage—elbow-deep in batter. There was a feast to prepare after all and with the blow to my head, I didn't want to overextend myself. *I should tell them I'm sick, and call it off.* But, I wanted my kids to have a perfect last Christmas with me. One without their mother behind bars. I sighed heavily while kneading the dinner rolls into shape.

As I laid a dish towel over the dough to rise, I couldn't help but stare at the door. I would have to have everything ready, with no excuse or reason to go near the garage while my in-laws were here. This meant I would have to go back into that freezer to get the turkey. *Should have left it out last night, damn it.*

I took a deep breath and readied myself for what I might see. I did cover him, but who was to say I wouldn't get a glimpse? *What does a dead body look like anyhow? He's been in the ice box, so I have to assume he looks purple.* The door to the garage clicked as I turned the knob and swung it open.

There was an eerie feel to the room. The air seemed hollow, making it difficult to breathe, and it was too quiet. I peered back over my shoulder into the house. Chatter from the girls upstairs and Shawn in the den hummed, but this room was still. I stepped down onto the cold concrete floor—my bare toes instantly numbing—and turned to look at the freezer.

If I didn't know any better, you'd think it was full of nothing but food. That is, until I saw the smear of dried blood on the handle.

Panic ensued, causing me to scan the room in a frenzy. As I suspected, there were more splatters. It wasn't much, but it was there, glittered on the wall behind the freezer. In my bludgeoned stupor, I didn't think about the mess. All I thought about was my head, and making sure it wasn't slit open like it'd felt.

In fact, as I came down the stairs this morning, I wasn't watching for a mess from my own tumble. I was too busy fixing my hair to hide my gash.

With that, I darted from the room and raced from the front foyer. I didn't know if I should be happy or peeved that there wasn't a mess. *Fucker must have cleaned up before trying to hide me.* I realized, *who does that!?*

I gave a deeper inspection and noticed the blood in the grout and smears of a hastily cleaned puddle. Giggles from upstairs made me jump. Clearly, my nerves were shot and I wasn't in the best mindset. Either way, it scared the shit out of me and reminded me of why he would clean it up. He couldn't let the kids know.

As I stood there fondling my busted hairline, I assumed the events that took place. Daryl tossed me, nearly breaking my neck. I was knocked unconscious, leaving him to think I was dead—*mor-ron*—he then took me to the garage to hide me and cleaned the mess before getting me in the freezer. It made sense that he would take those steps. The freezer was huge and packed full. It would be a hell of a task to empty, giving me time to wake up.

Speaking of, I still needed that damned bird.

I fiddled with my fingers as I went back to the garage, peeking in on Shawn as I did. He was busy playing one of his console games and paid me no mind. With the girls busy upstairs and my baking on hold for a moment, I went to get the turkey.

The more I thought about it, I couldn't remember where I'd placed it. I couldn't remember much from last night. Including the fact that I didn't put everything away and I now had thawed food on the floor, wasted. Luckily it was bagged, but still. Especially this time of year, it was a shame to see so much be thrown out.

After I procrastinated with the garbage and cleaned up the blood, I stood in front of the chest freezer. I still wasn't ready, but I needed to get this done. Or did I? Was it fucked up to serve a meal that sat next to a body? *Maybe I should just buy a new bird.*

Then again, it was Christmas Eve—would there even be one left? And the crowds, *oh my god the crowds...*

No, I needed to use what I had.

I removed the boxes and pulled on the door. The suction fought against me until it opened with a pop. The smell of frost nipped at my thankful nose as I peered in on my husband. To my shock, I didn't bury him as well as I'd thought. His hands were visible. So was the violet shirt he'd been wearing. I was however sure to cover his head. His bloody, mangled head.

There wasn't enough money in the world to make me remove the ground beef, french fries, and pita bread that hid him. I was there for the turkey anyhow, *so where is it*, I asked myself. I moved a few things by his legs when I saw the top of the wrapped bird. It was wedged under Daryl's frozen knees, stuck under rigor mortis and frost.

"Well, Shit," I murmured, *I guess we will be going to the store.*

Hello, Hello

Ha! and I thought getting a turkey on Christmas Eve was going to be the hard part. Little did I know it was going to be getting the kids in the car that proved to be the real struggle.

Shawn was lost in a fantasy world and the Girls were deep in a game of Barbies. No one wanted to leave their posts—not to mention my mother would be there in the next few hours, and they begged to wait and stay with her.

"We can't wait—the stores are going to close soon."

I pulled my SUV out into the driveway so they wouldn't have to walk past their father, but they didn't listen and came through the garage. I cursed under my breath and ushered them into their seats.

"I don't get it. We already have a turkey." Shawn complained.

"No we don't" I lied.

I automatically felt horrible; I don't think I'd ever lied to my children. Things were kept age-appropriate, but if they asked I told them.

"Yes we do, I was there when you picked it up." Shawn unbuckled his seatbelt before I could stop him and hopped out. "It's in the freezer."

The world around me seemed to slow, and sounds echoed. *Oh god!*

"No!" I screamed far louder than I needed to. Shawn froze in his tracks and turned around. The petrified look on his face told me mine was mean and aggressive. I did what I could to compose myself, glancing around to see if any of my neighbors saw my outburst before looking back at Shawn. "That one's not big enough..." I lied again, my heart sinking. *Why is it so easy to lie to you?*

He sulked back to the car but stopped and asked if they could stay home, *with Dad.*

"Dad went away for work again, remember?" Georgia peeped up.

"Oh yeah," His shoulder sank even more as he crawled back into his seat. "What about Grandma? She should be here soon. Can't we wait and—"

"No," I said for the umpteenth time. "The stores are closing soon. You're coming with. Now stop it, and let's go."

As suspected, the shops were cram-packed full of last-minute shoppers. My poor kids were pressed up against me like sardines in a can. There were no more turkeys in the size I needed, so I got two smaller ones, and ignored Shawn's logical banter. "Ok, Sure bud, if you say so," I kept replying.

I had no energy to cater to him and his observations. I was sick of it. I wanted to get home, finish my dinner prep, and go to bed—possibly cuddle with my mother, though that would be highly out of character.

By the time we returned home, it was time for a late dinner and bed. My mother would be there to tuck them in, then spend the day with them tomorrow.

As my children ate, I couldn't help but fiddle with the gouge in my hair, that was when I realized; *I have no answers for what happened to my face.* When the kids asked, I said I had an accident, and that's why you have to be careful on the stairs. Would I be able to swing the same half-truth to my mother without her catching on? That woman could read me like a bold font.

A knock at the door caused me to jump and grip the collar of my shirt in fear. I moved to see it from the kitchen, watching from down the hallway when it opened and my mother stepped in.

"Hello, Hello." She beamed, lugging her suitcase in behind her. "Where are my babies?!"

At the sound of her voice, my children leaped from the couch and raced toward her. Literally climbing over one another. They attacked her with hugs and kisses as I took her bags and moved them out of the way.

"Heya, Mom." I smiled. When she caught sight of my face, she gasped and covered her mouth.

"Mommy fell down the stairs, that's why you have to be careful," Elli spoke up.

"Did she now?" Mom narrowed her eyes and sneered. "Was your Daddy home when she *fell*?"

"No?" Georgia answered, confused. "Dad's been gone on a work trip."

My mother sucked on her bottom teeth, still not believing the story—which I luckily didn't have to tell—but she was willing to drop it while the kids were there.

Once they were asleep, it was a different story. We sat in the kitchen while Mom sipped on her warm milk. She was sitting in the breakfast nook as I puttered around the island, finishing up the last of my prep, while also keeping myself between my mom and the garage.

"You might be able to trick the kids, but seriously Jen. What happened to you?

"It was a freak accident, honest." I lied, "I was at the top of the stairs, I turned around to leave and suddenly I was waking up at the bottom."

"What were you leaving?" she asked taking another sip.

"Huh?"

"You said you were turning to leave, leave what?"

I choked, unsure of how to answer. "I, uh, changed my mind."

"About what?" She put her mug down and crossed her arms.

"My second glass of wine." I shrugged, hoping that would be enough to end the interrogation.

She shook her head and pursed her lips. "I smell bullshit."

"Mom!" I snapped and looked over my shoulder to make sure none of the kids were snooping.

She matched my shrug and stood up. "I'm going to bed, we have an early morning ahead of us."

A.TWISTED

56

He Hated You

I finished what prep I could and set an alarm for first thing. *I'm cutting it close*, I groaned while crawling into bed.

My mind reeled over the past 24 hours. It felt like a lifetime, but also, seconds. I was calm, yet panicked and though I knew how this was going to end—or at least pretty sure how—I wasn't bothered.

There was always the possibility of getting away with it, so long as things went to plan. Too bad, the idea of keeping it secret until I could move him churned my stomach and I still needed to get him to the dump. *That won't be suspicious at all*, I rolled my eyes. *I'll have to get it out of here before he's due home. Say the power went, and all the food spoiled... something—yea.* That way, he's long gone by the time anyone comes looking.

I shuddered at the imagery and curled deeper under the covers. *These are not Christmas-y thoughts.* I growled, *fuck sake. I hate this.*

The clock on my bedside table said one AM, and I was still wide awake. I tossed and turned, flipped my pillow to the cold side, and at one point positioned myself with my ass in the air. There was no getting comfortable, not with the anxiety that squeezed my ribs.

My lips flapped together as I let out a long breath. I would need to get up before my mother and keep her from snooping. There was really no reason for her to open the freezer, especially with so much junk on top, but with the way my luck has been lately, I wasn't willing to risk it.

Since I wasn't going to get any rest, I crawled out of bed and dawned my house coat. When I did, I noticed the blood crusted to my collar from my head smacking off the floor. My fingers fiddled with the pokey fabric as I silently told myself to take it off before anyone woke up. For now, it kept me warm on my way down to the kitchen.

As I piddled away, doing my best to time things out to have it dinner done, together, and on time, I couldn't help but watch the garage door. It haunted me as I peeled potatoes and tossed them in a pot to soak. I baked pies and set them aside to cool. Put the presents under the tree, and did anything else I could reheat when it came closer to crunch time. It didn't matter how busy I made myself; that freezer was screaming.

Slam! Slam! Slam! The sudden knock at the front door caused my soul to lurch from my body. I nearly yelped, I was so scared.

"Who the heck?" I asked when it rattled off again.

My mind instantly went to the police and panic trickled in. *No, there's no way they know. Not yet.* Plus, officers were required to announce themselves. No one was calling out.

My nerves were shot all the same, and my knees wanted to buckle. *Get it together*, I told myself while straightening my shoulders.

I ran to the front door, ready to yell at whoever thought it appropriate to knock at 4 AM on Christmas morning.

"If you're not freaking Santa Claus!" I started as I opened the door.

As soon as the lock clicked, the door burst open and a tall, slim brunette barged in. I quickly glanced out onto the street for witnesses to her outburst—happy to see there were none. What with it being so early on a Christmas morning, any sane person would be asleep in bed.

"Where is he?! Daryl!" The woman spun around, glaring. "He picked you, didn't he? You used the kids against him, I bet! You sick bitch." Her face was burned with tears, and her eyes were red and puffy. "He hates you, you know. Hates you. You should hear the things he says about you. If he picked you, it wasn't for love. He loves me."

I couldn't get a word in. The only thing I could do was grab her arm when she went to go upstairs and snap at her to shut up. As I stood between her and my home, my arms fanned like a goalie, I snarled.

"Who do you think you are?!" Coming over here like this?! I'd ask if you had any class, but seeing as you date married men—"

"Divorced men! You two have been separated for months!"

"This is news to me!" I crossed my arms and leaned back, looking her up and down.

She looked nothing like me—which I guess is to be expected—her short brown hair was silky smooth, not a crimp or a curl. Her high cheekbones and perfect nose made my face seem bleak. Oh, and don't get me started on my body. She looked like a twenty-something supermodel.

My haggard, well-worn body could never compare. I wasn't an unsavory woman, but I had meat on my bones and a bent nose from a baseball to my face as a child. My body carried and fed three healthy babies, and I had a stress zit forming on my brow.

"Oh, bullshit!" She snarled, clearly not trusting me over the cheating husband. "Daryl! Get down here you coward!"
With me in her way, she turned and pushed her way into the parlor.

I'm not sure what she expected to find in there, it's not like he would be hard at work so early. Then again, I'm not sure whether she knew what she was doing either. She tossed her purse on his chaise lounge, clarifying her plans to stay, and turned on me. Her eyes blazed hot with anger as she pointed.

"If you think I won't fuck up your family's Christmas, think again!" She hissed.

I raised a brow, *Oh really*.

"Tell me where he is!" Daryl's mistress demanded.

"He's not here! He's on a work trip." I lied better than expected.

"No, he isn't! That trip was with me, and he went to speak with you before we left. I've rescheduled our flights three times. Now, his phone dinged here! Where is he!?" She stomped her feet like Elli does during a tantrum.

Dinged? My jaw dropped. *She has 'find my iPhone' for Daryl's phone? What the hell?!* I had nothing to say; I was stunned. Even when we were happy, he would never give up his privacy like that to me. *Maybe we were never happy...*

"I know he's here!" She added, charging at me.

... Now that I've thought about it, I'm sure she was simply trying to leave the room, but at the time, I panicked and pushed.

The bimbo in her thin high heels tumbled backward, bending her ankle. As she fell, the corner of Daryl's solid cherry wood desk cracked her in the temple, splitting her head wide open and spewing blood across the floor. Her glazed eyes stayed open, and her chest stopped moving.

"Oh God..." I huffed.

Hot Meals and Good Comapny

"Mommy?" The sing-song sound of Elli at the top of the stairs sent me into a frenzy.

There would be no putting her back to bed now, and soon the other two would follow. So, I backed out of Daryl's office and closed the doors. For the first time ever, I wished he'd installed a lock. Now, the cardinal rule of staying out of this room would have to be my only insurance that she wouldn't be found until I got a chance to dispose of her.

Dispose of her, ugh. The idea of having two dead bodies in my home was too much. My stomach turned and I nearly wretched, but I swallowed deep and smiled at my daughter who stumbled sleepy-eyed down the stairs.

"You should be in bed, Santa won't come if you're up and moving" I lied, hoping she would be sleepy enough to listen.

"He's already been here." She pointed to the living room where the tree sat buried in presents.

Shit, why do I need to be so on top of things? My eyes widened and I wracked my brain on what to do. *Should I just take Elli into the kitchen and keep her busy? Can I even do that? How long does it take for a body to smell..? Oh my god, what if it starts to stink when his parents get here? They are supposed to arrive in twelve hours...*

"Well," I said, clapping my hands. "We can't go opening any without your Grandma and she needs her rest, so let's do something else. Hmm, I still have cookies to bake and icing to color. You want to help?"

"Oh! Yes, yes please!" Elli bcamed.
The rest of the morning dragged on now that I had two rooms to fear. I couldn't even enjoy the gift exchange. So much so, that my Mom told me to focus, *'they're only young once'* she'd said. Which didn't keep my mind from wandering.

There was a very good chance I was about to miss out on my children's lives. That this was going to be our last Christmas together. *When they learn what I did, they're going to hate me.* I bit back on the burn of tears in my throat and tried my best to smile along, boosting with the kids as they got everything they wanted—and then some.

Soon enough, every present was opened, and my family room looked as if there'd been a war between bows and wrapping paper. The kids went off with their new toys and my mother and I got to work cleaning up.

"When do Cindy, and Kenneth get here?" My mom asked, "Do they know Daryl is not going to be around?"

"I told them," I answered, monotone.

Keeping up a conversation was not something I was capable of at the moment. All I could do was think of all I would miss out on—how my children would feel, and how they will likely be placed with his parents over my Mom.

"And they don't care?"

I shrugged, "Cindy didn't seem to mind. She put up with the same sort of thing with Kenneth."

"Doesn't make it any better. If my husband did something I didn't like I would want my child to learn from it, not follow suit."

Once the living room was back in order, my mother joined me in the kitchen for some leisurely cooking. She made her remarks about my sleepless night, and how as odd as it was; though 'it sure did make for an easy day'. I wanted to scoff but bit my tongue instead. *Easy day? Maybe for someone who didn't just kill two people.*

Every bone in my body ached to tell my mom what I'd done, to get some kind of comfort. But I couldn't risk her being an accessory if I didn't get away with it, not to mention; who's to say she would comfort me and not lose her mind?

I honestly couldn't tell you what I would do if I were in her shoes. I want to say I would hold my child and tell them it'll be OK, but that'd be a lie and I didn't want my mother to have to do that—or look at me differently.

No. I needed to keep this to myself.

....

When the dreaded knock came, mayhem ensued as my children clamored to their grandparents. They climbed them like they did my mom, laughing, and giggling from being tickled.

My mother and I met Daryl's parents with fake smiles, and I gave loose hugs. They gave their holiday greetings and handed the kids each a few gifts to open. All three dropped to their haunches right there in the foyer and started ripping at the paper.

They were given lavish gifts—far too expensive—making them cheer about how they were the best grandparents ever. Even though they'd said the same thing to my Mom hours prior. We shared a look and Mom snickered, unbothered by their reactions. We were both, however, bothered by the gifts. I mean, who gives a six-year-old a laptop?

"You said you wanted to become a writer, didn't you?" Cindy asked Georgia; who looked just as confused as the rest of us. "Oh, she said she wanted to be a writer this past summer after reading some of the books I gave her."

I looked at my little fibber and puckered like a fish. She shied away but said thank you, and that she can't wait to be a best-seller. The Kids left us to our adult conversations, snickering about Georgia's lies.

"Dinner will be ready in half an hour," I grinned and ushered the adults to the living room.

"Lovely décor, as always Jen," Cindy said, making small talk.

Cindy and my mother both took seats while Kenneth stayed standing, clearly uncomfortable with the lack of male counterparts. He grumbled and groaned before asking if Cindy was driving home. When she said, yes, he nodded and mentioned getting a beer.

I promptly stopped him and said I would grab it. He tried to say it wasn't necessary—his way of trying to leave the room—but I insisted, forced him to sit, and rushed to the garage.

This was going to be harder than I thought. There wasn't a doubt in my mind Kenneth was going to try and sneak off to the parlor, and I couldn't let that happen. *I need to feed them and get them out of here,* I thought, but I knew they wouldn't like eating and running. *I will need an excuse. Something to make them leave. But what?*

Luckily for me, I didn't need to come up with a reason for them to leave. Kenneth did that for me by having two beers before dinner was even ready. Then a rye with his meal. He wasn't exactly belligerent, but Cindy was far too proper to let him be bored any longer.

So, they packed up, said their goodbyes, and left long before I expected. We all waved from the door—my smile officially genuine—as they drove off, not to be seen again until Easter.

How Do I Do This?

That night, after I put the kids to bed and said goodnight to my Mom, I snuck downstairs to the parlor. I hadn't a clue what I was going to do, or how I was going to do it, but I needed this room to get cleaned, and her corpse out of there before it started stinking up the joint.

I detoured to the kitchen to grab garbage bags, paper towels, all-purpose cleaners, and rubber gloves. It wasn't going to get rid of the crime, but it would hide it from the naked eye.

With my arms full of cleaning supplies I rushed to Daryl's office, peeking around corners like some kind of intruder. I moved swiftly, tip-toeing my way down the hall. It was late, but I'd only just said good night. Anything could happen. There was no surety that the heads on pillows were actually asleep, but I was in a pinch and needed to get started.

Still, my body froze outside the sliding doors, unable to go inside.

"How do I do this?" I whispered.

My stomach already wanted to erupt, and my hands shook with such intensity I nearly convulsed. There was no telling what kind of scene I would walk in on. The mess. I'd only seen bodies on TV or funerals with painted faces. The idea of seeing the gruesome scene—and having to clean it up—scared me.

My heart pounded and the room around me started to spin. I closed my eyes and focused on my breathing, going as far as to lean forward and place my hand on the door to support myself. *I have to do this. If I don't, I'm going to jail for sure.*

With that, my hand moved to the side, pulling the door with it. It took a moment to gain the courage, but eventually, I opened my eyes. The lights were still on and the electric fire blazed. It should have been a warm and inviting room, but there was an eerie chill in the air. I took another deep breath and was met with the stench of human excrement and copper.

Slowly, my eyes made it to the floor by the desk, settling on the woman's feet. It was nearly impossible to gaze any higher. I wasn't ready to see the aftermath of what I'd done. Which was going to make things rather hard to clean.

I forced myself to take another step into the room, closing the door behind me. Again, I wished there was a lock as I turned to face my problem head-on.

To my morbid delight, the majority of her body was on the area rug, allowing me to move the desk and roll her up like a burrito. My muscles strained as I wrapped her, but I pushed past the pain, knowing I had no other choice.

The small amount of blood that pooled on the hardwood was thick and gelatinous. I used a roll and a half of paper towels and a whole bottle of cleaner. The discarded tissues filled a small trash bag, and I tied it tight.

With the room back in order—minus the wrapped corpse—I went to take the bag to my outside bin. That's when I saw the black car parked on the street. My housecoat fluttered in the frigid wind while snow fell into my untied boots. My ankles were numb and I should have gone inside to finish up, but I needed to see.

It didn't seem to have anyone inside, and it was coated in snow from the day's fall. I recognized it. It was Daryl's old car. The closer I got, the more I was sure. The thing is, he sold that car nine months ago when he upgraded. I tilted my head at the tiny plastic succulent hanging from the rearview mirror when an realization set in.

Snow kicked up as I scurried back to the house to the parlor. The purse Daryl's mistress tossed was still on the chase. I snatched it up and dug for a set of keys. When I found them, I took them to the window and clicked the unlock button.

The lights on the car lit up and I nearly puked. *Oh fuck, now I need to get rid of a car too. Oh shit.* My knees went weak and I needed to take a seat. There wasn't an inch of skin that didn't tingle as I looked at the rolled-up rug.

How do I do this?

He Would Have To Wait

After a small panic attack and some contemplation, I had myself a plan. The question was whether or not I could enact it. Only time would tell, and I didn't have much of it. *I need to hurry...*

With a better idea of what I was about to do, I raced from the office, closing the door behind me. I took two steps at a time upstairs and quickly got dressed in all black. I tied my hair back in a tight bun and grabbed my shower cap from the master bath. It hugged the top of my head as I made my way back down to the foyer.

I put on Daryl's jacket, boots, and gloves before putting my own in a reusable grocery bag from the closet. His clothes were bulky, causing my arms to puff out beside me as I shuffled through the house to the garage. Its door beeped and rolled on its chain until it was open.

The street was still empty as I scurried to her car and got in. The smell of her cheap perfume choked me while I backed up the drive, and closed the garage door behind me. While there, the freezer called to me again, but I knew better than to try and move a frozen body tonight.

He would have to wait.

I was making good time, but did my best not to let it go to my head. I was neck-deep in this mess and needed to stay focused.

While still dressed in Daryl's outerwear, I started dragging the rug from the parlor to the kitchen, to her car. It was a heck of a struggle to get her bony frame through the house. Her body had become solid with rigor mortis, making corners an obstacle.

It took every muscle in my body to lift her, and there was an audible crunch when I forced her into the trunk. It caused me to cringe but that didn't stop me from making her knees to bend.

When the door was finally closed, I brushed my hands together as if a job well done and went back into the house to check for any messes. There were some smears here and there, but nothing a new bottle of cleaner couldn't handle—and thanks to my OCD tendencies, I had one.

Now came the *real* hard part—I needed to leave, and potentially never see my children again. Not without bars between us.

I went to each of their rooms and gave them all a kiss. Georgia stirred, making me flinch back, but she stayed sleeping, thank goodness. With my goodbyes placed, I went down to the car and headed out, stopping at the trash bin to grab the soiled bag from my original clean-up.

The plan was to go three towns over and leave her car in a no-parking zone. Once the car is towed away, it will be placed in an impound until the owner is contacted. Which will be rather hard considering I planned to toss her phone out the window on the way, but not before removing the sim card and tossing it too. All I'm praying is that they will put her car in the back of the lot and not notice a smell until summer, at the very least.

If I can get all of that done and home before the kids woke up, I would be laughing, but I doubted that to be the case. I didn't exactly have a way home, and I couldn't risk taking a uber and having any kind of paper trail.

I would need to take the bus system and from the little I knew about it, it was clearly a shit show. Even if it wasn't and it ran fluently, it will take all night and four different transfers to get home. Plus a thirty-minute walk in the snow.

I wasn't even sure if the buses would be running on Christmas night, but with it being such a large city I assumed they would.

There was nothing pleasant about this night, it tarnished what was supposed to be a beautiful time of year, and it infuriated me. *Why couldn't they have just gone on their vacation and left us alone? Why did they need to cause such a mess? They've ruined everything—I ruined everything. Why did I pick up that bat? Why did I shove her so hard? I did this. Why was I blaming them?*

Because it's easier I suppose. It was always easier to blame someone who isn't around to defend themselves.

I gritted my teeth as I whizzed through empty streets and sparse highways until I got to a fast food joint whose dumpster wasn't locked up. I pulled Daryl's hood over my head and got out to toss the bag of bloody paper towels.

With that bit of evidence gone, I drove a few more blocks to a lower-class neighborhood where I hoped there would be less security. The car slowed to a stop alongside the curb. I peer around, wondering how long it will sit here before she gets towed away. Then gave a silent prayer that it's left alone for a while, giving her some more time before the investigation starts.

I took off Daryl's coat and tossed it in the back before grabbing mine out of the spare bag and putting it on. With the hood still over my face, I got out and started my walk to the downtown core. From there, I got on the first of many buses, making myself homeward bound.

As I sat in the back row, I couldn't help but wonder if I'd done the job well enough. It's not like it was something I ever planned to do. So did I do it right? Or did I only make things worse. I should have called the cops the moment she hit her head, but I couldn't risk it. They would have asked too many questions and I wasn't a fluent liar—despite my actions the last few days.

I would have slipped up one way or another and wound up behind bars on Christmas Day. *No, I made the right choice.* Doing it this way gave me more time with my babies. Possibly a whole life if I play my cards right.

Here We Go

"I just thought it'd be nice," I explained to my mother as I packed random items from around the house." There are families in need, and we have more than enough."

"But furniture?" She asked, puzzled.

"It's an old chair from the den and the freezer. I wanted new stuff anyway," I lied. "Will you sit with the kids while I drop it off?"

"It's New Years!"

"The less fortunate don't stop needing things on the holidays, mother." I sneered, "I will be home long before dinner. So will you?"

"Of course, I will," She said, though clearly not impressed. "I just thought my time here would be spent together, but if you must do this, rather than hire someone, so be it. Miss independent."
I smiled and continued adding odds and ends to the box in my arms.

With someone to watch my kids, I went to the local hardware store and rented a van. This was one of the riskier parts of my plan, which left a trail... I gritted my teeth during the whole interaction, right up til the time I turned the key in the ignition.

From there, I did everything I could to calm my breathing and focus on the road. Which was hard with the way my mind reeled over the possibilities of today. Just like the other night, I could be pulled over, searched and be locked away. Sure, they had no reason to search my vehicle, but who's to say they wouldn't find one?

I did have the suburbia soccer mom look on my side, but even then, it wasn't foolproof. I have never been able to talk my way out of anything. Big or small.

The way my nerves reacted without a body in the back didn't hold promise for my ride to the dump. It was as if my ribs were closing in on my heart with the way they squeezed. I'd never felt anything quite like it. I couldn't breathe at times and even wondered if I was having a heart attack.

"I'm not cut out for this," And I wasn't. I'd never so much as gotten a detention in school let alone a murder charge.

After what felt like forever, I made it home and backed into the garage. The first thing to go into the van was the freezer, and thanks to the dolly I rented, I didn't need to call for help—though it would have been nice to have some.

Once it was secured in the back, I took the wheeled contraption to the den and got the chair, then the boxes I'd packed. It took all but an hour to get it all loaded and ready to haul off. So, I went inside for a drink break.

"Shawn wants to go with you, I said I don't see a problem with it," Mom tells me from my pantry. She was cleaning as always.

"Well, wasn't that nice of you? Next time say it's up to me OK?" I sneered.

"Sorry?" She raised her brows in shock.

"No, I'm sorry, I'm on edge."

"Why?" She stopped tidying and gave me a look of disapproval.

"It's been a morning, that's all." I took a deep breath and pinched the bridge of my nose. "Look, it's best that he stays here. I have no patience today."

"That's fine. I'll tell him, you just go get it over and done with. I'll make dinner."

"You're a lifesaver! But I'll tell him," I gave her a kiss on the cheek and went to say goodbye to the kids. I gave them extra big kisses and told Shawn the trip wouldn't be fun anyway. Plus the dump stinks, etc. I said we would all go on a day trip soon; and if he wanted just 'us' time, I could work that out too. Hopefully.
With my farewells in place, I headed out.

Snow and ice crunched under the tires as I backed my way down the driveway onto the street. I wasn't a hundred percent sure how, or why I was suddenly so calm about everything. I wasn't this person. Yet here I was, cool as a cucumber, traveling with a body in the back.

I turned the corner onto the highway, heading a town over to where the dump was. It was further out in the country, making my trip longer than my mother was expecting. *I will need an excuse,* I thought to myself. *Play off on my bad day, I guess.*

I shook my head. Not only was I too relaxed considering everything going on, I was becoming a mastermind when it came to lying. *Who are you?* I asked the eyes in the rearview mirror. I certainly wasn't the same woman I was a week ago.

As I pulled up to the gated entrance, my body numbed. There were cameras and though it wasn't my license plate, this is where that paper trail became a problem. Even if I tilted my head, or wore a hat, my signature would be the nail in my coffin.

The truck ahead of me inched it's forward to be weighed and I followed, stopping at the service window. *Here we go,* I gulped.

"Household waste, yard waste, or furniture? Hazardous waste?" The man behind the glass asked.

"Uh, furniture," I answered, not looking him in the eye.

"Stop on the scale, when the light turns green head straight there will be a break in the road, go left, follow it to the end, dump there, come back, get weighed again, pay, and off you go. Got it?"

"Straight, left, all the way to the end. " I nodded.

"Good stuff." He waved me forward.

I coasted ahead, feeling the bump as I landed on the scale. *Huh, that was easy enough,* I grinned.

When the light turned green I moved on and followed the man's direction. That is until I saw the Hazard sign. It sparked an rebellious thought and rather than go the way I was told, I turned and crept my way over a small hill.

From the top, I saw barrels, and bags as far as the eye could see, with a small area to turn your car around. I kept my foot on the brake as I slid down to the bottom, my heart pounding the entire time. *Don't wreck, don't wreck.* I begged the universe.

Luckily, I came to a stop at the edge of the drive and pulled a tight U-turn in order to face the back doors to the rest of the garbage. The pungent odor of chemicals attacked my nose when I cracked open the door. It was barely breathable.

It caused me to choke, and cover my mouth and nose with my hand, hoping to filter the air. It didn't work. The stench breached my fingers and caused my eyes to water. *Jesus, what is over here?*

It took a moment, but I gained the nerve to move my hand and breathe heavily through my mouth. There was little I could do to save myself from the putrid stank, other than hustle to get this over and done with.

The ramp slid out no problem, and the dolly once again came to the rescue. I pulled the freezer out, and made it a point to tip it over near the hillside, watching it fall further—deeper—into the toxic waste. It landed with a crunch, and I turned back to close the doors. I wasn't dropping the rest off here, I was truly going to donate it. It was a stop I planned to make on my way home.

The drive back was a little less nerve-wracking. As far as I was concerned, they were gone. When they do find Daryl's mistress, they will link it back to him. By then, I will have a missing person's report made up, and be playing the part of the worried wife to the best of my ability.

When they come knocking I can say, *"I assumed he left with her—now it seems he fled."* Or, something along those lines. In reality, I won't say anything without a lawyer.

There will have to be someone in her life to confirm they were dating, and by how hostile she was with me, they likely knew her plans to confront him the other night when he didn't leave with them. It all played into my plan. I could play dumb, and blame it on a dead man.

"Wow, I may actually get away with this..."

Happily Ever After

"Look mom! Decorations!" Elli smiled as she helped her grandma make New Years streamers.

"Your trip took longer than I thought it would," My mother added, not looking up. As I suspected, she had her panties in a knot from me being gone so long, again, when we were supposed to be having family time.

"I'm sorry, I had things to get done."
I rolled my eyes. I wasn't in the mood to deal with her snide remarks.

"Errands and donations are not more important than time with your family. I'm only here for another two days," Mom complained.

"You live in the next town over—It's not like we never see you," I added, taking off my coat and boots and putting them by the fire.

"Oh, so that makes it OK to bail on me all week." She tossed the streamer she was taping and crossed her arms like a bratty child.

"Don't start a fight with me in front of Elli. She sees it enough with her father." I urged.

"And who's fault is that?" My Mother raised her brows, testing me to argue.

"I'm going to go before I say something I'll regret." I clenched my teeth as I left the room.

"Good, go shower, you smell horrible."

··············

The piping hot water felt like heaven, as did the loofa I used to scrub the day off my skin. I couldn't recall whether or not I'd showered in the last two days. In fact, since Daryl's murder, things were a blur.

The way my skin changed color the more I scrubbed, told me I was filthy and likely smelt worse than the dump. What looked like a tan washed away to reveal my pasty-white legs. It was disgusting. I turned my nose up at the dirty water, ashamed that I'd let myself slip so far. *Maybe I wasn't handling this as well as I thought...*

For good measure, I added more body wash to my hand and lathered it up in the ruffles of my loofa to start all over again. Next was my hair, then face. As my hands circled my cheeks, I couldn't help but replay the events again and again. It was like the water was pouring them over me, wave after wave. Tears burned, and a lump lodged itself into the back of my throat.

I glanced at the bathroom door and decided that there was no better time to let myself feel. So I did.

The build-up within my chest erupted as tears poured down my already-soaked face. At times, I wasn't sure if it was the fear of being caught and spending a life in jail, but the longing I had to go back in time to change what I did, crushed me. *I never should have talked to that lawyer,* I cried louder. If Daryl never got that bill, we wouldn't be in this mess. If I'd watched my mouth, and not poked the bear...

Sure, he would have left me with nothing, but the kids would have been taken care of, and that's all that mattered. I would make do, I always did. Now, I didn't know what was going to happen, or how I would keep myself out of trouble.

Sooner or later, they would find her body and I would need to lie out my ass, and still, there may be evidence to suggest I did it. It's not like I knew what I was doing or what to watch out for. My freedom was on a clock, and I didn't know what time it was.

When all was said and done, I stepped out into the steam-filled room and sat on the toilet to trim my nails and pumiced my heels. I was in no rush. My kids were taken care of downstairs, and with everything I'd done, I knew I needed to cherish every moment like it was my last. That included self-care.

I stood up and wiped the mirror clean. My eyes were dark and sunken in, my cheeks were thinning and my face was paler than usual. *Jeez,* I sighed. *I'm definitely not handling this like I thought.*

The air in my master bedroom was frosty compared to the muggy warmth of the bathroom. It nipped at my naked skin as I got dressed in silk PJs and headed downstairs for dinner. I yawned as I walked out of the room. I was already ready for bed, and it was barely 6 PM.

There were still hours to go before midnight, and even then who's to say how late the kids would stay up. My body automatically started to ache, and I wanted to skip the rest of the day. I wanted to go to bed and leave the festivities to my mother—I'd clean up the mess in the morning—but there wasn't a chance in hell that would fly.

The formal dining room was decked out in handmade and store-bought décor. It was busy in the most beautiful way, and definitely had Elli's touch. As I took my seat at the table, she greeted me with exaggerated, 'Happy New Year' and bounced in her seat.

Shawn was already there, munching on pickles and cheese, while Georgia played on her new laptop. She was actually quite enthralled with writing now that she was doing it.

"Dinner is served," Mom announced as she walked in carrying a fat juicy roast, surrounded by steaming potatoes. My mouth instantly watered, and my stomach ached from being hollow. The kids clearly felt the same way. Each one stopped what they were doing, and swooned over the platter in my mother's hands.

She placed it on the table between all of us and began to carve. Georgia closed her computer and put it off to the side. Elli got to her knees and leaned over the table to get a big whiff, as Shawn licked his lips.

The moment each one got their plates, they dug in. They attacked their food as if we starved them and this was their first or last meal for a week. In all honesty, that's just how good my mother's cooking was.

When it was my turn to join in on the barbaric feast, the phone rang.

"Ignore it," my mother told me, glaring. "You're with your family."

"It's New Year's. It's probably family calling," my chair skidded along the floor as I got to my feet. "Heck, it could be Daryl," I added for the sake of it.

"Ha!" My mom scoffed. "I doubt that very much."
She sat down to her own plate and I left the room to grab the cordless phone off its dock.

"Hello?"

"Jen?"

"Yes, this is."

"It's Nackton, Jaremy Nackton."

"Oh," I said, recognizing the name of my P.I. "One second, let me go somewhere more private," I said, stepping into the den. Once I was out of earshot, I froze.

What was I supposed to ask? It's not like I needed dirt on Daryl anymore. Maybe I should see if he saw anything over the last few days. *Shit. He could know everything and be calling to blackmail me.*

Throughout my crime spree, I never once thought about my P.I keeping tabs. *Shit, shit, shit.*

"So, I have some good, news, or bad depending on how you look at it." he said nonchalantly. "But from what I've learned, I think it's for the best..."

I let out a deep breath, "OK, Let's start with the bad news." I didn't want to wait—*Just tell me what you know!*

"Well, turns out he *was* leaving you, and the kids... uh, it also looks like he was taking the money."

"Oh?" I already knew this, or at least I was pretty sure I knew.

"Yea. He has a bunch of money in an offshore account, plane tickets. A villa in Tuscany... Looks like he had someone on the side he planned to run away with." I waited for Jeremy to tell me something I didn't know, but my silence was assumed to be sadness.

"You OK?" He asked after a moment.

"Yes, Um. What's the good news?" I asked, looking over my shoulder. *My mother is probably fuming right now.*

"Good news is, according to your Prenup, I have everything you need to take him to the ringer before he disappears. You can fuck up his whole plan," The man laughed before clearing his throat. "Excuse my language. Uh, the file will be here at the office, I'm not back until the second though. But it's there. If I were you, I'd give that lawyer of yours a call."

I said thank you, made plans to come by Thursday to pick up the papers, and hung up the phone.

The room around me spun, forcing me to take a quick seat on the couch. Now, if the cops came knocking, I had proof that he was fleeing. Sure, he didn't use the plane tickets, but who would after a murder? He would drive south like any sane person. Right? *Maybe that's what I should do... Just take the kids and go. I wonder if there is a way to tap into those accounts of his?*

I went back to the dining room, ignoring my mother's grumpy glances. As I took a seat with my family, my mind wondered; there were so many different ways this could all play out. I could come out of this unscathed, or I could lose everything and spend the rest of my days behind bars.

Either way, the cops will eventually arrive at my door—that's for certain—and when they do. We won't be here.

"Hey mom? What do you think of Mexico?"

The end.